I call you Dr. Della.
We had lots of fun
community center.

Introduction

The founding members of the Sisterhood of Purple™ have been depicted as three whimsical characters for the past twenty years. Most of their lives have been spent complimenting a line of greeting cards. I did not even give them names because I wanted you, the reader, to apply their expressions and messages to your mom or grandmother, sister or well-loved aunt, or your special friend.

In my mind, "the girls" developed full-fledged personalities, and eventually needed names, especially for my gift books. As I was thinking about names, a childhood memory popped into my mind. I recalled summer camping trips with my family near the magnificent Three Sisters mountains in my home state of Oregon. The nicknames for the mountains, Faith, Hope, and Charity, fit perfectly; I knew in a flash I had found names for my characters.

With virtues as their names, I could blend deeper inspirational messages into my theme of encouraging women in their daily lives.

Enjoy Faith, Hope, and Charity in their escapades as they live their lives with light-hearted humor and a touch of whimsy, delivering nurturing and uplifting messages.

Faith, Hope, and Charity's individual bios are available at the back of the book.

Girlfriend Wisdom
Live, Laugh & Love

Written & Illustrated by
Jody Houghton

The Sisterhood of Purple
Supports, deepens,
And values friendships;
Grants permission to giggle
And joyfully scream
With the voice
Of the little girl within;
Accepts and honors
The changes and growth
On our life's journey
Together.

Honorable Society

The Sisterhood of

DURPLE

May your life be a

BOLD ADVENTURE

May your days
be filled with

GALES of LAUGHTER

And may you love

BODACIOUSLY!

LIVE
LAUGH
LOVE

To honor

A girlfriend
Brings heart-felt
Joy.

To honor oneself
Fills the heart
To nourish the joy.

When My Friends And I Are Old, We Shall Wear Purple.

We will spend our Saturdays seeking out every
garage sale within a ten-mile radius.
We will critique the bargains and say,
"Oh, remember this,
my grandmother used to have one of these!"
We will grocery shop all about town,
hunting down the sales and tasting
deli samples at each stop.
We will make promises to each other:
never wear plastic rain bonnets,
never wear nylon knee-hi's with a dress,
and always keep a pen and paper
next to our beds so we won't forget
those night-time thoughts.
We will have a cup of tea at dusk, gossip a little
and giggle a lot. We will do all these things
and more, my friends and I,
when we grow old and wear purple.

**L**ife is a great big canvas. Throw all the paint You can on it.

Each new day is an opportunity to create something special in what might be called just another day.

Last week my friend Hope and I were shopping. We didn't really need anything, you know, just shopping. We strolled into our favorite dress shop. We were both amazed at the marvelous display of colors ~ a wonderful shade of red with a complimentary shade of lavender, enhanced with a spring green and detailed with red and white hearts. We were so drawn to the colors that we had to buy something.

As I was buying a blouse with these fabulous colors, Hope called to me from a flowing display of scarves.

Hope, tossing her head high...

wrapped a scarf around her neck; she looked like one of those cute models on the home shopping TV shows!

Hope was beaming like the brightest star in the universe. I felt so proud of her! It might simply have been a new scarf, but looking at my friend in that moment took an ordinary, "just shopping" day, and splashed rich vibrant colors on my life's palette.

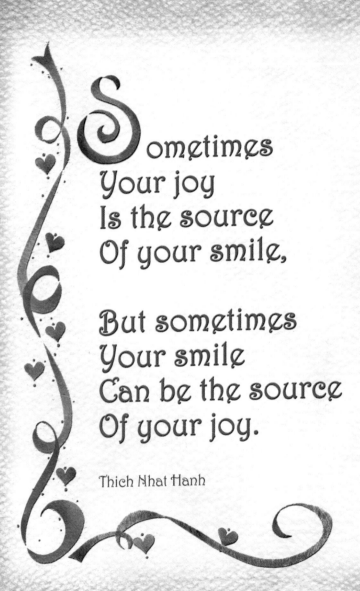

Sometimes
Your joy
Is the source
Of your smile,

But sometimes
Your smile
Can be the source
Of your joy.

Thich Nhat Hanh

Two

Roads diverged
in the wood,
and I took
the one
less traveled by,
and that has made
all the difference.

Robert Frost

LIVE
LAUGH
LOVE

The Boldest of the Bold Award

is an honor received by members of our
Sisterhood of Purple group for addressing
the element of boldness in our lives,
for living a truly bodacious life!

Today, I am honored to
announce that our sorority
sister Faith has won
this award!

Faith's courageously
bold hat design
earned our respect
and recognition.
We took ever so
many pictures
to remember
this occasion.
Her time in
the spotlight is
now a story
to be entered
into our chapter's
memory book.

Let me give you every detail ~

Let me tell you how wonderful, I should say, "bold," Faith is. She went to our local arts and crafts supply store and went up and down every aisle- I'm sure that's what she did because she had a little bit of everything on that hat.

It was adorned with beads, rhinestones, peacock feathers, swirls of fabric tied into bows, glitter paint, flowers, and a little dough-art frog sitting on the edge of a leaf.

It was a chapeau beyond the grandest des Chapeaux.

She even glued a little vase to the brim to hold water so the flowers would stay fresh and perky all day. She is truly creative.

After Faith graciously received her award, she bent down and took a box from under the table. In the box were all the left over craft supplies and treasures from her creation. Arranged on a family heirloom silver platter, presented with a sense of royalty, were purple-handled scissors, glue sticks, and all the necessary tools to share her collection of treasures.

The tray was passed from table to table.

A delightful frenzy permeated the room, punctuated with ooh's and aah's and all manner of joyful noise.

"Take what you like, and pass it on," Faith said loudly. She was barely heard over the cheerful sounds in the room.

A little sparkle and glitter can add a whole new dimension to your day.

All the craft supplies Faith used on her award-winning hat were now being enjoyed by everyone in the room. Each person embellished their own hat designs. Hats twinkled with purple rhinestones and dangled with bugle beads, peacock feathers waved and ribbons danced among the flowers and glitter.

The Sisterhood of Purple was a glamorous site to behold!

The Joy in the Sharing,
brought a richness to our
time together.
What a great example of
a life well-lived:
passing on a kindness
to others and making
an ordinary day
extra-ordinary
for all.

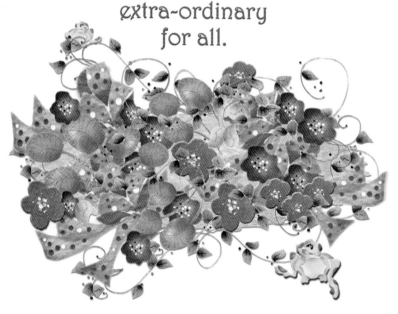

The best and
Most beautiful
Things in the world
Cannot be seen
Or even touched.

They must be
Felt with the
Heart.

Helen Keller

My Phenomenal Friend

...is a wise teacher who
Supports me through
Life's Lessons.
She is a fairy godmother
And has given me the
Power to Dream.
She reminds me to listen
To the whisperings
Of My Heart.
The love in her smile
The twinkle in her eyes...

She's a
Phenomenal
Woman.
A Phenomenal
Friend.

(Especially when she
dances in her slippers)

A Hat Statement

A hat speaks for a woman
As she enters a room.

A big hat with
A stately crown
And wide brim, speaks
Of courage and
Self-Assurance.

A small hat ~ a beret,
A pillbox, or a pretty
Hat with lots of lace ~
Speaks of patience
And charm.

A hat is a smile,
Or shows determination;
It expresses a mood
For its wearer.

A hat speaks volumes
Before a word is spoken.

Melody Englund

FRIENDS
for laughter,

PURPLE
for eccentricity,
and a

RED HAT
for ATTITUDE!

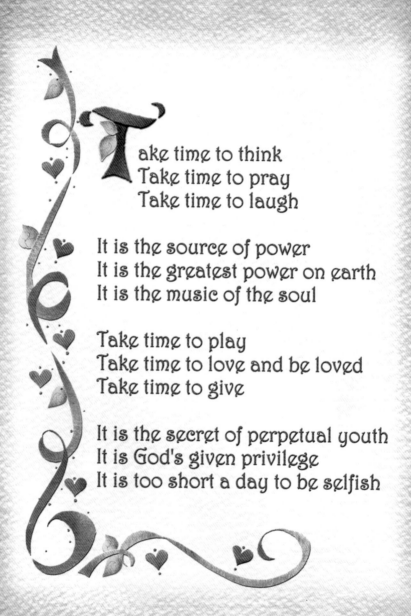

Take time to think
Take time to pray
Take time to laugh

It is the source of power
It is the greatest power on earth
It is the music of the soul

Take time to play
Take time to love and be loved
Take time to give

It is the secret of perpetual youth
It is God's given privilege
It is too short a day to be selfish

Take time to read
Take time to be friendly
Take time to work

It is the fountain of wisdom
It is the road to happiness
It is the price of success

Take time to do charity
It is the key to heaven.

On the wall at
Sisters of Mercy
Children's Home,
Calcutta, India

There really are so many things I want to do in the course of a day. Life is busier than ever, and time keeps flying by.

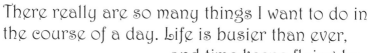

I started writing my appointments in a pocket calendar; it is a great way to keep track of my daily events.

Before I got in the habit of using mine, I would worry about missing lunch dates, or the hairdresser. I bought a beautiful calendar with uplifting messages, and I love using it.

Before I started using my calendar, I frequently showed up at the wrong place on the wrong day. I'm still not perfect, but now when I am misplaced, I am open to whatever marvelous surprise life has prepared for me.

I have met the most wonderful people in the midst of a "surprise."

Last week, Charity and I were meeting our high school friend for lunch. We arrived at the Café On The Hill at twelve o'clock sharp. Our calendars both confirmed our appointed time and place. We waited and waited. The hostess was watching for our friend, whom I described as shortish, about my age, with kind of brownish short hair. The very helpful hostess kept bringing over the most friendly women, all with brownish hair and all about my age. The only problem was, none of them were our long-time friend.

The hostess finally brought us someone we did know. It was Faith! We weren't scheduled to have lunch with our dear friend Faith, so we were very surprised to see her.

Faith was meeting a friend of hers at the same café. She pulled up a chair and we chatted as we waited for our friends. Faith looked at her calendar, looked again, and exclaimed, "Oh my goodness, I thought it was Wednesday and now I realize it's only Tuesday!" We all laughed and shook our heads. "What a blessing that we are all here. Let's have lunch!" I exclaimed. So we did.

As we were dining on our Veggie Quiche, Faith remarked, "This is great quiche, and I get to come back tomorrow. What a nice bonus.

Life is full of great surprises!

When I got home, my answering machine was blinking with a message from my friend. She remembered writing the time and date of our lunch on the back of a check deposit slip, but then she used it to make a deposit at the bank. She couldn't remember if our date was this week or next week and asked if we could schedule a time for next week.

I chuckled and thought to myself, "How perfect; I guess Hope and I will have a bonus lunch as well. We're going to Café On The Hill next week too."

LIVE

I could not
At any age,
Be content
To take my place
By the fireside
And simply look on.
Life was meant
To be lived,
And curiosity
Kept alive.

Eleanor Roosevelt

LAUGH

The person
Who can bring
The Spirit of Laughter
Into a room
Is indeed
Blessed.

Author Unknown

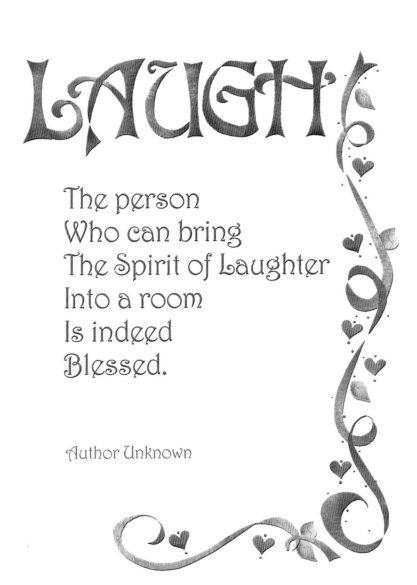

LOVE

Love is the golden thread
That ties our hearts
And souls together.

~

Love is patient,
Love is kind.

~

Tell me who you love,
And I'll tell you
who you are.

Mother Teresa

Love is a fruit in season
at all times, and within
reach of every hand.

~

We can do no great thing;
only small things
with great love.

~

Intense love
does not measure;
it just gives.

Women's Auxiliary Meeting TODAY 3:00 p.m.

Faith, Hope, and I volunteer to help with a project in our community ~ a giant size project, a wonderful dream.

The dream is to make a hand-made quilt for every new mom who delivers a baby at our community hospital. We believe hand-made gifts are always Made With Love. Our work is very important! The quilts could become keepsakes and be handed down generation after generation.

Each and every stitch would be made by hands and hearts of women who love sharing their time and talent.

Several women in our group are quilters and knew just what was needed to begin our special project. We looked at quilt patterns and talked about shapes and colors.

We chose a Crazy Quilt design. It represents the expected and unexpected events in life and a positive outcome for each of them. Life isn't always bright and beautiful. We have all experienced some of life's challenges and feel qualified to pass along sage advice to younger women. We planned to embroider Words of Wisdom from members of our group around the border of the quilt.

My friends and I are in a Cleaning and Clearing Stage of Life, so we decided to donate the fabric. We searched our closets, attics, and sewing room shelves for yardage from projects once started, but never completed.

Hope was embarrassed to find four yards of cornflower blue cotton meant for a long hippie skirt she had planned to make.

The sales receipt read: July 15, 1968!

The natural blue cotton would be soft and comfy for our quilt.

She clearly had no desire to finish a hippie skirt.

Although, that fabric brought back some great memories!

I found some curtain panels in my sewing room, made of natural gauze with sweet yellow flowers that would look lovely surrounding a baby's face.

I purchased the panels before my decorating preferences blossomed into deeper, richer colors, like purple.

Now I am going to paint the room purple with a dazzling color wash of sparkling pearl-white.

The sweet yellow flowers will look charming on the quilt, especially with Hope's cornflower blue.

At our first meeting to work on the quilt,
we cut our fabrics into small pieces.
We tossed the pieces on the floor,
creating a grand array of colors.

Piece by piece,
stitch by stitch,
our dream became
a reality.

As we completed our first quilt,
you could have heard a pin drop in the
room; it was a sacred kind of silence.
We were passing on our sweet memories,
making something new and meaningful
out of something we no longer needed,
yet was special in its own time.

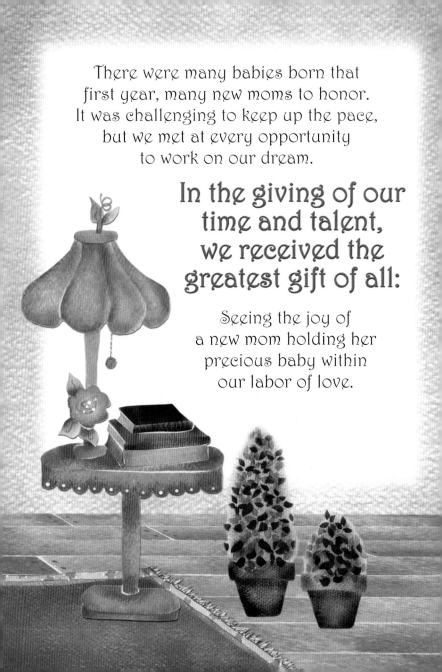

There were many babies born that
first year, many new moms to honor.
It was challenging to keep up the pace,
but we met at every opportunity
to work on our dream.

In the giving of our time and talent, we received the greatest gift of all:

Seeing the joy of
a new mom holding her
precious baby within
our labor of love.

Right now her heart is full and her life
is bright and beautiful.

We are grateful our gift of love will be
there to give sage advice when
it is most needed. We imagine her
in the future, on a challenging day,
suddenly noticing the Words of Wisdom
we embroidered along the quilt's border.

We can envision her peaceful
smile as she remembers the special day
when she received the quilt from some nice
ladies at the hospital.

Girlfriend Widsom resides
in all of us;
in living our lives
to its fullest,
in expressing heart-felt joy
with laughter,
and in loving one another
more deeply each day.

I hope you have enjoyed
stepping into the lives
of Faith, Hope, and Charity.

Blessings,

Jody

Faith's Bio

Hope loves to talk about her true blue friend: "Faith is such a worker! She simply doesn't believe in just dreaming about something, or merely talking about it; she has to make a list, get organized and start right in baking, getting flowers from her garden, or making phone calls. Whatever it takes, Faith's on the job and no job is too big. If you need a mountain moved, she's your gal! She calls it her passion; her work ethic comes from her heart and brings her great joy. You will definitely want Faith on your team!"

Faith's mission is to encourage others to believe in what they can't see. She recognizes the reward for heart-felt work is to succeed in your beliefs. Faith declares, "My dream is that everyone will know the great and mighty strength that comes from God. Every person deserves to live his or her best dream."

LIVE
LAUGH
LOVE

Hope's Bio

"Hope will always put a smile on your face with her encouraging words," says Charity, Hope's devoted friend. "She can shine a light in the darkest places. Of course she's the most optimistic person I know; tell her any challenge and she can give you more ideas and options for success than you can ever think of on your own. We never want to lose a friend like Hope ~ she keeps us all going."

Hope's mission is to encourage others to see the bright side of life and recognize they can achieve their hearts desires. Hope is quoted as saying, "Sometimes my encouraging voice sounds like a cheerleader, and as a matter of fact, that's how I imagine God ~ cheering me on as I accomplish all kind of things I didn't know I could do. My dream is that everyone would know this kind of solid support and assurance."

Charity's Bio

Faith is quite vocal about Charity's near sainthood: "Charity is very patient and always kind. She is never jealous or rude. Charity always thinks of others. She celebrates life every day. Charity is the best friend you will ever have because she will never, ever stop loving you or letting you know just how special you are."

Charity's mission is to spread all the love around this world that she possibly can! She believes she can spot the goodness in anyone after only three minutes of conversation. "There is something to love about everybody." says Charity adamantly, "If you look for the good, you can grow it into love. You can quote me on that because it's the truth! My dream is that everyone will see the good in others and experience great love."

Jody's Bio

Jody Houghton's illustrations and writings have warmed the hearts of dedicated readers for over twenty years. She draws on her personal life experiences, spiritual values, and her peer group - wise women over fifty - in creating her books.

Jody is a native Oregonian. Her life is blessed with two wonderful children, Michele, and Iain, as well as the unconditional love of their little dog, Coco.

Enjoy Jody's other books, published by Zondervan's Inspirio gifts:

ISBN:
0-310-98537-4

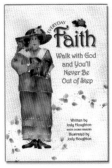

ISBN:
0-310-98570-6

ISBN:
0-310-98811-X

ISBN:
0-310-98812-8